EVANGELISM IN RURAL AREAS

HOW EASY IS IT?

TABLE OF CONTENTS

INTRODUCTION

One of the most difficult tasks confronting the small church is that of evangelism. Of all the various ministries of the church, it is this portion of the ministry that seems to be the most difficult and unproductive. Week long evangelistic services that once attracted many people within the community now attract only the faithful few. Home Bible Studies, which are effective in the larger communities, find only moderate success in the smaller communities. Door to door evangelism, popularized by Evangelism Explosion, not only is unappealing to the congregation, but seems an exercise in futility by those who do attempt to institute the program.

CHAPTER ONE

DEFINITION

Evangelism: Evangelism is the announcement, proclamation, and/or preaching of the gospel (1 Corinthians 15:1-4), the good news of and about Jesus Christ. Therefore, the gospel is a communicated message—communicated in verbal (Luke 7:22; Romans 10:14-17) and/or written (Luke 1:1-4) form.

Rural Area: Rural area or countryside is a geographic area that is located outside towns and cities.

Evangelizing in Rural Areas

One of the most difficult tasks confronting the small church is that of evangelism. Of all the various ministries of the church, it is this portion of the ministry that seems to be the most difficult and unproductive. Week long evangelistic services that once attracted many people within the community now attract only the faithful few. Home Bible Studies, which are effective in the larger communities, find only moderate success in the smaller communities. Door to door evangelism, popularized by Evangelism Explosion, not only is unappealing to the congregation, but seems an exercise in futility by those who do attempt to institute the program. Friendship evangelism seems the most promising, yet, in most rural communities, there appears to be more friendship than evangelism. Everyone in the community knows each other, yet there are few who respond to any evangelistic thrust. While the pastor, who has the gift of evangelism, may experience some success, frustration and discouragement come when he attempts to motivate and involve the rest of the congregation. If the strength of the small church is found in its fellowship, its weakness is discovered in evangelism. To overcome this weakness, the church needs to not only realize the importance of evangelism as the major thrust of the ministry of the church, it also needs to develop programs that enable the church to accomplish the task.

Evangelism in rural areas today is gradually given way to a robust and fast-growing community of faith, with elements of joys and sorrows, problems and plans, the successes and failures (how easy is it?). It helps us to understand better the growth of social, intellectual, political and material development brought to the people of the rural area. The social, cultural and political problems hampering Nigeria's quest for unity and appropriate human development have become major staples of contemporary concern of the rural Evangelism in Nigeria (Obinna, 1995).

The multi-dimensional aspects of Evangelism rural areas in the various facets of the Nigerian Society have received the attention of the Church and still beckon on the Church for dialogue, critical and constructive dynamism if the church must continue to be relevant today Evangelism and into the future. Indeed the history of the Church and Evangelism in Nigeria does not make full appreciative sense without a decisive entry for the better into the economic, cultural and socio-political development of the nation (Onwuanibe, 1995). Only with such vigorous engagement for the authentic progress and development of the nation can the Church's message be welcome in the seeking of solutions to emergent challenges facing the rural areas. Ultimately, human development is about the realization of potential. It is about what people can do and what they can become--their capabilities and about the freedom they have to exercise real choices in their lives.

1. To identify to what extent the Church Evangelism can contribute to community Evangelism in rural area.

2. To determine to what extent the Church has been vital and relevant in community Evangelism of Nigeria.

3. To determine the problems of development still facing the Church and how it can still contribute to rural area in Nigeria.

- Has the Church played any role in rural Evangelism in remote area in the State?

- To what extent has the Church been relevant rural Evangelism?

- How easy is it?

To determine and study the various roles the Church has been playing in rural evangelism in Nigeria. It is restricted to the socio-economic, cultural and political roles of the Church especially in Eastern State.

Among the limitations include: time, resources, human factor, limited data, information, culture and tradition (such as Oro festival during the day).

CHAPTER TWO

CHURCH AND EVANGELISM

This chapter focuses on those areas of concern, the Church has always seen as problems facing evangelism in rural area and which it has tried in history to help provide solution to. The Church, through her social teachings, has joined in the social struggle to fight the limitation of carry evangelism assignment and bring better life for the people. This chapter, therefore, specifically reviews literature related to the Church and how easy it is, the Church in moral and value orientation, the Church in Education, the Church and human development, conflict resolution and peacemaking, healthcare delivery and development, the Church and socio-economic concerns, political development, gender mainstreaming and gender issues, the Church in scientific and technological development, the Church in social work and charity, and development challenges facing the rural evangelism in Nigeria today.

The Mission of Evangelism

To be effective in evangelism, the church needs to recognize that the proclamation of the redemptive power of God to a lost and dying world is the heart and soul of the church ministry. Evangelism is neither an option, nor a luxury of the church. Christ gives this mandate to the church on two different occasions. In

Matthew 28:19,20 Christ states, "Therefore go and make disciples of all nations, baptizing them in the name of the Father and of the Son and of the Holy Spirit, and teaching them to obey everything I have commanded you. And surely I am with you always, to the very end of the age." His final words to the apostles in Acts 1:8 reiterated this directive, "But you will be my witnesses in Jerusalem, and in Judea and Samaria, and to the ends of the earth." To state it bluntly, every church that is not aggressively involved in the evangelization of rural areas in which he/she lives is failing to be disobedient to the command of Christ. In being obedient to the great commission, it is important to realize that evangelism is not to be equated with conversion. Evangelism is the communication of the gospel message to a lost world (the Greek word meaning to proclaim or announce good news). Conversion is the realization of Christ's redemptive power in the life of the individual. Evangelism is the process while conversion is the end result. Evangelism is the task of the church, conversion the task of the Holy Spirit. The church is commanded to evangelize the world. Therefore evangelism is the heart beat of God.

Obstacles to Evangelism

In developing evangelism in the small church, there needs to be an understanding of the obstacles that will be encountered.

1. Exclusivism. Because the small church consists of a close circle of relationships, it can easily become exclusive to outsiders. Whether intentional or accidental, when the church no longer welcomes new people into the body, the church will become hindered in evangelism. To be evangelistic, the church needs to be willing to assimilate new people into the life and fellowship of the church.

2. Law of privacy. The smaller the community the more people know about the activities, problems and lives of one another. As a compensation for this, within smaller communities, an underlying value is that each individual is to respect the privacy of the other by not asking them questions of a personal nature. Since ones' faith and beliefs are extremely personal, it is often difficult and considered impolite to talk to others about spiritual matters. In order to avoid offending their neighbours with whom they live in close proximity and depend upon, they avoid talking about the gospel.

3. Previous decisions. In many smaller communities, people have been previously exposed to the ministry and beliefs of the church. As a result they have already made the decision not to attend.

Marketing techniques, which are effective in larger communities, have little impact in smaller communities.

4. *Past history of the church and individuals in the church.* People in a small community often remember the past history of the church and people who attended. This knowledge of the past becomes the basis by which they judge and evaluate the church. If the church has had problems in the past or if individuals have had problems with members in the past, people will form a negative perspective of the church. This negative perception then hinders any outreach attempts with that individual.

5. *Discouragement.* If the church becomes focused upon the result (conversion) rather than the process (evangelism), then the church can easily become discouraged regarding evangelism. When people share the gospel and see few results they can become discouraged. Like Ezekiel, the church needs to be reminded that the body is to be faithful in communicating the message of redemption regardless of the reception it receives (Ezekiel 2:5-7; 3:17-21; see also Jeremiah 2:17ff Isaiah 6:9-13). The gospel needs to be continually proclaimed even if there are no visible results.

Communities in Nigeria have been bedeviled by numerous challenges of Evangelism in rural areas which include: severe economic, political and social crises, decline in the standard of education, moral and infrastructural decay, cultural crisis predicated on the fact that traditional values in the people's cultures have been heavily impacted by materialism, science and technology and ideologies. Health facilities are in total decay.

All these problems call to question the role of the Church in rural Evangelism still contributing to the provision of needed succor in these problem areas. In view of these problems and issues, the big question is the relevance of the Church in the present situation. Since relevance is an important feature of any meaningful phenomenon, event or institution, especially in the sphere of human life, the Church's role in the solution of problems in the 21 century Nigerian society may be definitive in the justification of its existence among the Nigerian people. Moving from the great signs of vitality and great contributions of the Church to community development since the advent of the early missionaries to rural areas of Nigerian, this work will look at the role of the Church to rural Evangelism in Nigeria today and set how it can help address itself to several problems of poverty and other social problems facing the people and see how it can further join the government and other stakeholders in bringing sustainable development among the people for which it was a source of hope in the past.

CHAPTER THREE

EVANGELISM AS A PROCESS

An examination of the ministry of Christ and the book of Acts reveals that Christ and the apostles adapted their evangelistic method depending upon the spiritual understanding and perception of the individual. Since evangelism is a process, the goal is to move people closer to an understanding of the implications of the gospel. This begins by assessing and understanding where they are in relationship to the gospel and then adapting the method to the individual.

1. The Antagonist. The antagonists are the individuals who have such a strong negative reaction to the message of Christ that they are openly hostile to Christianity. This hostility may be a result of their view of the gospel or perceived offenses they have experienced with Christians. Reaching these individuals for Christ begins with the demonstration of unconditional love that manifests itself in the acceptance of the individual. In this case the gospel must be communicated through actions rather than words, the goal being to break down the hostility so that the individuals are more receptive to the message of the gospel.

2. The Ignorant. The ignorant individuals are those who are unfamiliar with the teaching and implications of the gospel and scripture. Religiously they are ecumenical, viewing Christianity as one of the many ways to God. However they have little desire to know more about the Christian faith. The most important part of the process in reaching the ignorant is the cultivation of a personal relationship with these individuals in which love is unconditionally demonstrated. While the implications of the gospel should be carefully communicated, it should be done in a non-threatening, non-argumentative manner so that the individual will become a seeker.

3. *The Seeker.* Seekers are those who see themselves as "religious," that is they are familiar with the Christian beliefs and desire to know more. They are aware of the basic elements of the gospel but ignorant of the full implications. They are concerned about their "felt needs" and are seeking ways to meet these desires. They are seeking to know more about the Christian faith and the teaching of the Bible. Ministering to them involves meetings these needs while at the same time formulating opportunities to communicate the full implications of Christ's redemptive work so that they will desire to know more about him.

4. *The Examiner.* Examiners are those who understand the implications and personal demands of the gospel. They are aware of their sinful state before a holy God and are looking for spiritual answers to their spiritual needs. It is at this point that the witnessing process becomes persuasive in the proclamation of the gospel. The Examiner needs to be challenged to make a personal decision to accept Christ as there saviour.

5. The Responder. Responders are ready and willing to make a personal decision for Christ. When an individual responds to the appeal to accept Christ, the church needs to be able to assist the individual in making that personal decision and then be committed to the discipleship of that person.

Cultural Development

When culture refers to the cultivation of personal qualities in terms of intellectual, moral and physical attainments, it is personal culture. It is societal when it embraces the form of society as an artificial environment in terms of infrastructures and symbols of civilization (Onwunaibe, 1995: 61).

In the landscape of culture all cultures are not the same. Cultural anthropologists do not like evaluating one culture against another. They rightly do so since cultural anthropology in its perspective is descriptive and scientific. Cultures are graded high or low according as the principles of valuation are used to critically examine what makes for cultural development or progress or what retards culture. Hence in a tapestry of cultures of a given period or place, some of the cultures will be given high regard as compared with others according as they conform to the stipulation of the valuative principles which relates basically to the enhancement of human life in a genuine way. Culture is not merely material and physical; it is essentially the concern of the mind, of self-consciousness, of the spirit of man, which is the sphere of transcendence. A descriptive collection of cultural data with a view to generalization is at the scientific level. A cultural anthropologist may rightly place monogamy and polygamy on the same level of legitimacy, since they apparently serve their respective purposes in a given culture. The point of discussing the function of the valuative principle is its importance in dealing with the role of the Church in cultural development for the Church's stance is theological and moral. In the light of the discussion of the meaning of culture, cultural development means the quantitative and qualitative increase in the scope of the qualities, conditions and achievements.

which make further enhancement of human life considered from the reference point of human transcendence; for the authentic being of man is eminently spiritual and transcendent (Onwuanibe, 1985:62).

Man as a Cultural Being

The culturality of man is an important issue in intellectual discussion today. A pressing problem demanding solution is how man is not just a being in nature, natural being, like any other animal in the continuum of nature but a cultural being, who has the potentiality of going beyond the bounds of natural environment to create an artificial one in view of enhancing the quality of his life.

Man develops as man in culture amid nature. In the view of the Church, it is a fact bearing on the very person of man that he can come to an authentic and full humanity only through culture, that is, through the cultivation of natural goods and value. Wherever human life is involved, therefore, nature and culture are quite intimately connected (GS, 1988: 959). Man in all his humanity is not just a product of nature nor of history alone, but the amalgam of history and nature which is called culture (Mondin, 1985: 147). Man has the capacity for culture because of what Michael Landmann calls "anthropine gap." It is based on lack of specialization of man unlike animals which are specialized. As he put it: The point of departure is that man as distinguished from animals, has at his disposal neither specialized instincts nor organs highly specialized for particular operation. In contrast to animals, human, according to an ancient observation, at first seems badly equipped in fact, unfurnished and incapable of survival. This lack of specialization is called anthropine gap (Landmann, 1982: 126).

The lack of specialization of man should, however, not be considered as a merely negative quality. It is positively linked with human creativity through which man can create for himself the structures which he lacks by nature. For example, he cannot fly by nature but he creates for himself machines that help him fly in covering distance more than the speed of sound. Man has tremendously constructed out of the forces and materials in nature things to feed, cloth and shelter himself more than nature has provided for animals (Onwunaibe, 1995: 63).

Furthermore, the culturality of man is rooted in the symbolic faculty of his rationality. Man can distance himself from the concrete environment and rise to the representation of things in their absence; he can endow these representations or signs with additional values and meanings to create symbols; cultural development is expressed in symbolic form. The Church as a living reality, not only creates and uses symbols, symbols of Christianity, but also recognizes the symbols of a culture. The relevance of the Church in Nigeria can be seen in the adaptation of the symbols of Nigerian culture or cultures.

The Dialectics of Cultural Development

Cultures impinge on one another in cultural exchange. The impact may take on the form of opposition which may lead to the destruction of one or to integration. The term "dialectics" in this context, in its mild meaning, indicates the process of cultural exchange in which there is a kind of opposition either strong or mild and eventual integration. A dialectical movement is one in which there is a positive (thesis), opposition (antithesis) and a synthesis in which some elements of both agents or factors are preserved in a higher form at the level of reconciliation (synthesis).

Culture is a dynamic reality. The ability of a culture to face up to foreign cultures or elements of another culture and integrate them in the exchange of cultures assures its survival; otherwise atrophies (Onwunaibe, 1995: 65). A culture is critically selective as it appreciates what is good and lasting amid the fades and fashions of the time, and incorporates it in the mainstream of the fabric of the culture. It is creative in bringing about new forms or ways of living in the effort to enhance the quality of life of its people. It shades off bad forms or elements as it undergoes the process of change in acquiring good new forms in the process of cultural development. A major problem which arises in the dialectics of cultural development is the problem of preserving traditional values and of how to harmonize them with the advances in science and technology (Onwunaibe, 1999:

The Church in Cultural Development in Nigeria

The Nigerian culture or cultures have had the impact of Christianity for more than a century, and the influence of the Church can be seen in the landscape of the cultural development in Nigeria. The Church is trans-cultural in the sense that it does not identify itself wholly with any particular culture, since its mission is to bring the whole human race to salvation (GS: 43). Through the transcending vision of the supernatural perspective, the Church can always help in the renewal of cultures in their development. A local culture as in Nigeria can identify to a large extent with its local culture by making the Christian message permeate the local cultures and purify the cultural values of the local culture in the effort to integrate good elements of the local culture in its liturgy and in the Christian living of the People of God (Onwunaibe, 1995: 65). The beginning of the Church in Nigeria was slow and arduous, but persistent as these great missionaries, such as Fr. Le Berre, Fr. Joseph Lutz, Fr. Horne, Brother Herman and Jean-Gotto, Mr. Charles Townend and Bishop Shanaham courageously made their way into the hinterland to bring the light of Christian faith in Nigeria, especially in Eastern Nigeria in the early 1900s. Theirs was the thin edge of the wedge of the contact of Christianity with native cultures in Nigeria.

The impact of the Church could be felt in the dismasting of inhuman practices and institution such as slavery, human sacrifice, killing of twins and in the establishment of Christian villages which eventually gave way to schools for formal education. Translation of the gospel into the vernacular languages and the production of catechism in vernacular languages showed the good sense of recognizing the native culture, for language or tongue is a main vehicle of culture. Many local customs were banned as "pagan" and there is need today for inculturation, in terms of appraising and recognizing good traditional values.

Church in Moral and Value Orientation

There is a great cultural crisis in Nigeria today. Traditional values in Nigeria cultures have been heavily impacted by materialism, science, technology and ideologies (Aligwekwe, 1991). Such values as the sense of religion and God, sense of the dignity of man, respect for elders, honesty, honour, hard work, extended family solidarity, respect for life, personal and social religion, hospitality, justice and peace have not escaped the cultural influence of foreign elements (Onwunaibe, 1995: 68).

The cultivation of the dignity of the human person is the central point of reference in a culture and not material possession. Authentic cultural development is centered on the dignity of man which has imponderable value. The true model for progress is not one that extols material values only, but one that recognizes the priority of the spiritual. Great and rapid changes are taking place in the social fabric of many nations working together for a better future for their citizens. But no social change will constitute a true and lasting enrichment of the people if it sacrifices or loses the supreme values of the spirit. Development will be one-sided and lacking in humanity if materialism, the profit motive or the selfish pursuit of wealth and power, take the place of the values, such as mutual concern, solidarity, and the recognition of God's presence in all life. A growing sense of brotherhood, of social love, of justice, the banishing of every form of discrimination and expression, the fostering of individual and collective responsibility, respect for the sanctity of human life from its very conception to its natural end, the preservation of a strong family spirit--these will be the hallmark of successful development and the strength of the people as they move towards the third millennium.

The prospects of overcoming the cultural crises in Nigeria today call for the revaluation of cultural values of Nigeria in the light of the Church's mission and contribution towards the st21 century in

Nigeria. Such cultural values are religious sense, sanctity of life, family solidarity, social responsibility, truth, honesty, hard work, acquisition of wealth, justice, peace and love are to be purified and revalidated as being amenable to the Christian economy of social ethics. The problem of neo-paganism and traditionalism which ignores the cultural gains as a result of the influence of Christianity requires the immediate attention of the Church in terms of deepening the faith of the people by catechetical instruction and by inculturation (Onwuanibe).

Inculturation is an effective means for achieving meaningful cultural development. On this point Pope John Paul II spoke during his historic pastoral visit to Nigeria in 1982. Addressing the Bishops, he said: an important aspect of your own evangelizing role is the whole dimension of the inculturation of the gospel into the lives of your people. The Church today respects the culture of each people. In offering the Gospel message the Church does not intend to destroy or to abolish what is good and beautiful. In fact she recognizes many cultural values and through the power of the Gospel purifies and takes into Christian worship certain elements of a people's customs. The Church comes to bring Christ; she does not come to bring the culture of another race. Evangelization aims at penetrating and evaluating culture by the power of the Gospel (L'osservatore Romano: 12). This passage reflects the basic principles of inculturation in the Church and it is in full accord with the declaration of the fathers in Vatican II Council who declared: Living in various circumstances during the course of time, the Church, too has used in her preaching the discoveries of different cultures to spread and explain the message of Christ to all nations, to probe it and more deeply understand it, and to give it better expression in liturgical celebration and in the life of the diversified community of the faithful. The goodness of Christ constantly renews the life and culture of fallen man (GS: 58; Luzbetak, 1991). The above passages, which give the meaning of inculturation show the necessity of inculturation especially in a developing mission country like ours. A lot has been done to rectify the short-comings of early missionaries in Nigeria in terms of deeper studies in Nigerian cultures, in using the native tongue (languages) in the Church celebration etc. The problem of the st21 century Church in Nigeria with regard to culture is development based on originality of inculturation and in purifying native cultural symbolic institution.

The Church in Education Development

The history of the Church is strongly characterized by the flowering of intellectual progress in education at the primary, secondary and tertiary levels. The roots of modern education really run back to the intellectual revival of the twelfth century when the Church schools, especially in France deepened general interest in literature and facilitated the progress of physical and historical sciences (McSorley, 1944: 351). In the medieval cultural development or achievement the role of the Church can be seen in the establishment of cathedral schools at Paris, Chartres, Leon, Reims and Liege; these later developed into famous universities.

patrons of learning, art and science, for example, the Medici family in Florence, the Sforza family in Milan, the Este Lords of Ferrara, Alfonso the Magnanimous of Naple. The result was the creation of the famous Leonardo da Vinci's Virgin of the Rocks, Last supper, Mona Lisa, Michelangelo's creation of Adam, the Fall, the Last Judgement in Sistine Chapel and his scripture, the Pieta (Chester :351) Must people would agree that widespread illiteracy, low educational standard and inappropriate education contribute very significantly to African's economic and social problems (Kinoti, 1996: 51). Unquestionably, education is crucial to economic and social development and it must receive top priority in any serious attempt to find lasting solution to Africa's problems. Only education will give the people understanding, knowledge, skills and confidence necessary for life in the modern world.

Christian missionaries introduced modern education into Africa and despite their limited resources built some very impressive educational institutions. These institutions produced teachers, artisans and other man power for the mission and junior workers for the colonial government. In many African countries, practically all the political leaders who led Africa from colonial rule to independence and the administrators were products of mission schools and colleges (Kinoti, 1996:51). Good mission schools sought to produce Christians who had intellectual or technical ability as well as to mold the character of the pupils in order that they would become hard working, honest and caring.

Back home in Nigeria, by building schools which range from the primary to secondary levels, the Church recognized the importance of education in development. Some of the schools and colleges were of very high quality, for example, St. Gregory College in Lagos, St Patrick's College, Calabar, Christ the king College, Onitsha, Holy Ghost College, Owerri, College of Immaculate Conception, Enugu and Stella Maris College Port Harcourt. This tradition of education continued to flourish until after the Nigerian Civil War, when the government took over schools.

As an organization which is dedicated to the salvation of humanity, to the great good of humanity, the Church in Nigeria is justified in her claim to partnership in education. She has always been actively involved in education in Nigeria and rightly so (Onwuanibe, 1995:72

CHAPTER FOUR

DEVELOPING A WITNESSING COMMUNITY

Developing the church into a witnessing community begins, not with the development of evangelistic programs, but with the development of an evangelistic attitude within the congregation. To develop a witnessing community, the church must become obsessed with evangelism, otherwise it will always remain a program rather than a mission and passion of the church.

1. Prayer as the Foundation. Having a passion for evangelism begins with prayer. Before Christ sent out his disciples as evangelists for the kingdom, he first called them to pray for the harvest (Matthew 9:35-38). Prayer not only changes the spiritual receptivity of the lost, it also changes the attitudes and motivations of the believers who are called to witness. Without prayer there will be no passion for the lost, no power in the testimony and no presence of God in the message. To develop an evangelistic community, the people need to begin to pray specifically for individuals who they desire to hear the gospel of Christ.

2. Building Relationships. Having identified and begun to pray for specific individuals within the community, the next step in the evangelistic process is the building of a personal relationship with that individual. Approximately 75-90% of all people who come to Christ do so as a result of a personal relationship with a friend or relative. Peter writes to the churches in Asia Minor to be "always prepared to give an answer to everyone who asks you the reason for the hope that you have" (1 Peter 3:15). This implies close personal contact with people. This is especially crucial in the small church where relationships rather than programs form the backbone of evangelism. The first step in building redemptive relationships is to utilize the personal relationships that people already have with others in the community. People need to be encouraged to spend time with the unchurched, cultivating relationships and ministering to their physical, emotional and spiritual needs. One of the strengths of the small church its knowledge and awareness of the needs of people within the community. By ministering to these needs, the church can demonstrate the love of Christ that breaks down the barriers that the culture erects.

3. *Evangelism as a Team Sport.* To develop an evangelistic community it is necessary for people to realize that evangelism is not done by Lone Rangers, who, after converting one soul, ride off into the sunset in search of another. Typically, it requires five contacts with different Christians before a person comes to know Christ. Consequently, the evangelistic process involves the interplay between the individual Christian and the church community. Developing a personal relationship with people

involves assisting the person in developing personal relationships with other Christians within the community as well.

4. Personal Invitation. To be a genuine witnessing community, the church, and individuals within the church, need to clearly communicate the gospel to the people that they have developed relationships with (Romans 10:9-15). In witnessing to people, it is important to realize that the proclamation of Christ to the lost individual is not a one-shot affair. Rather it requires patience and gentile persuasion. The Church is not merely to be a place where Christ is proclaimed to the faithful, it is to be a community that is actively and purposely involved in the process of bringing people to the point of decision with regard to the redemptive work of Christ. While the church cannot "save" anyone, God has chosen his people to be an indispensable part of the process.

Respect for Human Dignity & Equality of Persons

The Church has always taught that the human person is the focus of development rural areas through evangelism, and all structures whether economic, social and all theories must be assessed in the way and manner they affect the human person and his dignity. In the sphere of economics and social life too, the dignity and entire vocation of the human person as well as the welfare of society as a whole have to be respected and fostered, for man is the source, the focus and the end of all economic and social life (GS: 63).

The human being should be the criterion of every social and economic activity because of "the sublime dignity of the human person, who stands above all things and whose rights and duties are universal and inviolable" (GS: 26). The basis of human dignity and rights is the human status of being created in the image of God, (imago *Dei)* when other parts of creation share only in the vestiges of God (vestigia *Dei)* as the fathers of the Church taught (Uwalaka, 1995: 99). Man as the summit and crown of creation is expressed by Christ when he taught that the Sabbath was made for man and not man for the Sabbath (Mk 2:27). Commenting on this the council fathers remarked that "the social order and its development must constantly yield to the good of the person since the order of things must be subordinate to the order of person and not the other way round" (GS: 26). The call of the council is that man being distinct from the material object ought to be treated as ends not as means as Kant taught because he was created in the image and likeness of God (Gen 1:27) who has made man little less than a god and with glory and honour crowned him (Ps 8:5).

Following the living tradition of the Church the Vatican II set forth the following principles to give socio-economic development the human face it deserves. According to the council the ultimate and basic purpose of economic production does not consist merely in the increase of goods produced, nor in the profit nor prestige but every economic effort is to be directed for the service of man, in his totality, taking into account his material, intellectual, moral, spiritual and religious needs irrespective of race *(GS:* 64). It taught also that to give respect to human dignity that economic development must remain under man's direction, not left to the whims and caprices of few people or nations nor the almost mechanical evolution of economic activity (GS: 65). It means that from a Christian point of view that the economy is not a simple market process regulating itself by the mere equilibrium of demand and supply in the market (Rauscher, 1991: 114). But instead "justice must be applied to every phase of economic activity, because this is always concerned with man and his needs" (Benedict XVI, 2009: 37). Human dignity also calls for duty. Therefore, all citizens have the duty to contribute according to their ability to the socio-economic progress of their own community (GS:

The Equality of Men and Women and All Peoples

Directly following from the dignity of mankind is the fundamental equality of all men and women since each person possesses an original uniqueness (Uwalaka, 1995: 100). The council taught that "all men are endowed with a rational soul and are created in God's image; they have then same nature and origin, and being redeemed by God can they not enjoy the same divine calling and destiny? There is a basic equality between all men and it must be given greater recognition." The council admitted that all are not alike as regards physical capacity, intellectual and moral powers but cautioned against any form of social or cultural discrimination in basic personal rights on the grounds of sex, race, colour, social conditions, language or religion since they are incompatible with God's designs. The theme of equality between men and women and all peoples is given classical formulation in the Pauline letter to the Galatians: "There is neither Jew nor Greek, there is neither slave nor free, there is neither male nor female: for you all are one in Christ Jesus" (Gal 3:28). In the right of this the Church has always stood for the right of everyone. In her magisterial writings she has always condemned acts of injustice against women. However, she acknowledges the inherent differences between men and women. The council also condemned excessive economic and social disparity between individuals and people of the one human race as scandalous and as sin against social justice, equity, human dignity and social and international peace (GS: 29). It therefore called for an abolition of the immense economic inequalities which exist in the world and increase from day to day' in order to fulfil the requirements of justice and equity (GS: 66). "Within a country which belongs to each one, all should be equal before the law, find equal admittance of economic, cultural, civic and social life and benefit from a fair sharing of the nation's riches" (CBCN, 1972: 12).

Universal Destination of the World's Goods

The Church also teaches that social and economic development should be made universal not just for rural areas. The argument is based on the fact that if there is a God who created nature and handed it to his children there is no doubt that his eternal plan is that it be for all present and potential members of the human race (Uwalaka: 1995 : 102). It is also based on the solidarity flowing from the universal brotherhood of all human beings since all peoples have God as their father. The Fathers and Doctors of the Church had taught that people are bound to help others especially the poor not merely out of their superfluous goods. In their words a needy person has the right to be helped out of the wealth of others. God destined the earth and all it contains for all men and all peoples so that all created things would be shared fairly by all mankind under the guidance of justice tempered by charity. The council taught that people should regard the external goods they possess not merely as exclusively theirs but common to others also in the sense that they can benefit others as well themselves (GS: 69). It called for a limit to personal acquisition and accumulation especially at the expense of the poor. In the axiom attributed to Gratian, the council tasked both individuals and governments to "feed the man dying of hunger, because if you do not feed him you are killing him." According to Uwalaka (1995: 102) "this is the whole story about liberation and option for the poor which is not option against the rich, but a fundamental option for social justice and love, for the human dignity and thsolidarity.

In teaching us charity, the Gospel instructed us in the preferential respect for the poor and the special situation they have in the society. The more fortunate should renounce some more generously at the service of others. If beyond legal rules there is really no deeper feeling of respect and service of others, then even equality before the law can serve as an alibi for flagrant discrimination, continued exploitation and actual contempt.

His Encyclical Letter *Sollicitudo Rei Socialis* (1987) is a document on social concerns. It gave a theological reflection on issues of global poverty and the ever widening gap between the rich and the poor which has given rise to the division of the human race into first world, second world and third world. He warned that such a situation seriously compromised the unity and universal brotherhood of mankind. It is not only individuals but also whole nations are rendered destitute while some nations are squandering the much needed resources on irrelevances and more painfully on weapons of mass destruction. He criticized the phenomenon of "super development" involving consumerism and waste that exist side by side with abject misery and indigence (Ibid: 27, 28). He went so far as to berate the superfluous adornment of the Church while millions of people hardly take their daily bread: "Faced by cases of need, one cannot ignore them in favour of superfluous Church ornaments and costly furnishings for divine worship; on the contrary, it could be obligatory to sell these goods in order to provide food, drink, clothing and shelter for those who lack these things" (Ibid: 31).

The Church is the Church of the poor and it is to the needy that we dedicate our services and our lives. But we recognize the need, on our own part, to make a humble examination of conscience. It is not sufficient that we be men of moderate personal expenses in our own private lives, we must also let it publicly appear to men that this is so. Our hearts are given to the poor and we accept that we must be careful to ensure that the poor see this and accept it as true. We must be careful that external appearances do not seem to give the lie to our private good intentions and that externals do not seem to align us with the powerful and privileged classes. In this, as in other things, it is Christ who must be our model… we direct our concern to the needs of the lowly ones, the poor in our land. They suffer many injustices and these injustices seem to branch out from one deep core or centre.

The Bishops also mentioned some of the Church's contributions to social justice. These include their pioneering role in education and health care. They tasked the government on holistic development of the people. They finally resolved to continue their dedication to economic and social development of Nigeria and to impress on all the need of just and equitable distribution of the national wealth (Ibid: 15, 16, 31).

Like the Universal Church, the hierarchy in the Nigerian Church has done creditably well over the last few years with regard to her discerning and teaching roles…. There are indeed various societies, committees and commissions in the Church that take care of the less privileged, the oppressed and the marginalized in society. The Church's commendable involvement in the Liberian Refugee Camp at Oru in Ogun State is well known.

But the author noted further that "yet, providing the succour for the under-privileged and victims of injustice is the realization of only one aspect of the social doctrine of the Church." He called on the Nigerian Church "to challenging the evil status-quo." He challenged the Church to respond to her prophetic calling in more practical ways than have been the case in the past (Ibid: 103).

Specifically, he asked the Church in Nigeria to emulate secular organizations that have taken over and are now in the forefront of the struggle for human rights and dignity in Nigeria by engaging in mass action and peaceful demonstrations (Ibid:105-112). To ensure that the goods of the earth serve both the poor and the rich John Aniagwu has also called for a similar action from the Church in Nigeria. "The time may well have come for the Church in Nigeria to borrow a leaf from the examples of the Philippines and Poland and take to the streets to drive home all her sermons about justice and human rights that have so far gone unheeded. It is to be understood that bishops, priests, seminarians and nuns will be at the head of the proposed mass action. There should be no dearth of laymen and women to march behind their spiritual leaders" (Aniagwu, 1995:15).

CHAPTER FIVE

Summary, Limitation and Recommendation

Summary

This project comes as a result of a great disappointment in the lack of evangelism in the rural areas here in Nigeria. In developing this project new ways and possibilities of evangelism were found that would draw the attention of people to Christianity and press on to deeper commitment to the church. This project aimed to help in finding new and better ways of communicating with unchurched people and opening the possibilities to preach them the gospel and make them disciples of Jesus.

This research material will help many pastors and evangelists in reaching people in rural areas, making them disciples of Jesus and active Christians in the life of the church.

Limitation

Despite all the negative information I have heard about evangelism in rural areas, I remain an obnoxious optimist about local congregations. One of the reasons I am so optimistic is that many of us are no longer ignoring the problems. One of the early steps to church revitalization is a willingness to "look in the mirror."

With that in mind, in this project I try to reach out in the mirror if their churches are not evangelistic. And here are seven factors that leaders may see when they get that honest perspective.

There is no priority of evangelism. I know. That sounds too self-evident. But churches that do not make evangelism a high priority are really making it no priority at all.

Many laypersons believe that evangelism is what we pay the pastors and staff to do. Such a perspective is first unbiblical and, second, unproductive. Evangelistic churches always have enthusiastically evangelistic laypersons.

Many churches have an excuse mentality. So pastors blame it on the laity. The laity blame it on the pastor. And both blame it on culture, the denomination, or some other external scapegoat.

Too many church members do not connect prayer with evangelism. Many members are pretty good at praying for those who have physical needs. But many are woefully lacking in praying for those who have the greatest need: a personal relationship with Jesus Christ.

Too many Christians fail to be compassionate and Christ-like to others. Evangelism always ultimately includes a clear articulation of the gospel. But too many Christians never get that opportunity to share the gospel, because they fail to show Christ in their actions and compassion.

Most church ministries are not intentionally evangelistic. The church should always seek to make certain any and all ministries include intentional efforts to share the gospel.

Recommendation

Many are involved in evangelism, but I have an uneasy feeling that very few Christians actually *"DO IT"*. Much evangelism that takes place within and outside our Diocesan setting is purely based on a short term rather than a long term view of the way the Kingdom of God should be extended. Everybody has heard of meetings or crusades in rural areas where many people have prayed the sinner's prayer, and genuinely decided to turn from ungodliness to living a righteous and holy life. However is this all that matters? Did Jesus tell us to go and make *decisions* or *disciples*?

Below is an outline or coded keys to effective evangelism in a rural areas that I think is workable.

We Must Bring People into Relational Communities

If evangelism is to be effective in rural areas, we must ensure that people are added to a Church. The aim of evangelism is the renewal and transformation of lives, not just to get people to pray the sinner's prayer. Salvation is a process that starts even before a person comes to Christ (through the drawing of the Holy Spirit) and continues after the decision is made to follow the Lord.

A new convert cannot function as a Christian apart from a local church, because this is the environment in which God has ordained for him to be nurtured and eventually find expression for his ministry. When evangelism occurs in an urban area, there are existing Churches for new believers to join. However, when evangelism occurs in a rural setting there may not always be established Churches to work with. What is to become of those who accept the Lord in such a situation? The evangelist or those conducting the evangelistic effort are responsible for these new believers. How can helpless newborn babes be left to fend for themselves? It is essential that these people be placed in *rural evangelism* so that their spiritual lives can be nurtured.

If we take a closer look, we will discover that there are several tremendous advantages to planting Churches. Here are just a few:

A. Church Planting Produces a More Holistic Approach to Evangelism

Evangelism is a sub-set of church planting. The wider aim of the extension of the Kingdom of God includes church planting as part of it, especially in areas where there are none. Evangelism is actually incomplete without the planting of churches.

B. Church Planting Leads to Church Growth

Even in areas where there are established churches, the planting of new churches increases the rate at which people are reached. Take for example a larger church which has reached a plateau in its growth. If this church makes an effort to plant new churches the Kingdom of God will be extended. At the same time more people will have the opportunity to become involved in ministry.

C. Church Planting Overcomes Barriers

Most people who live in remote rural areas do not have access to an established church. They either live too far from an existing church or they may belong to one of the many people groups that do not have a church witness in their midst. We need to plant churches in these groups so that they will, in turn, reach out further to others of their group. In this way the Gospel crosses barriers to those who may be beyond the reach of present evangelistic efforts.

D. Healthy Churches Plant More Churches

Just as Christians are supposed to make disciples of all nations, healthy churches should produce baby churches. This approach to evangelism produces a commitment to those who come to the Lord, as mother churches are in a position to care for their daughter churches. They will be nurtured and ministered to even if there are only a handful of new believers.

We Must Emphasize On Discipleship

Those with a short term view of evangelism are only interested in getting people to make decisions to accept Christ. Yet, one of the most powerful ways for the process of evangelism to continue is to disciple those who have made decisions for the Lord. As discipling occurs, **firm** and **stable** believers who understand the importance of reaching and discipling others are produced. The process of evangelism then becomes self perpetuating.

Our churches needs to develop a philosophy of ministry that views evangelism task as incomplete if we lead someone to Christ and then leave them, especially if they are from a remote rural area where there is no church. For this reason, we are to be committed to discipling new converts wherever the gospel is sent to. This should be done until the new converts can stand on their own feet and are gathered as a body of believers that is able to reproduce itself.

This philosophy of ministry is costly. We cannot accept all the opportunities that present themselves to us. Progress seems slow. But it is worth it. As new believers are discipled and a church is established, they will in turn reach out to others and start new Churches which they will care for.

We Must Develop Leaders

There is a two-fold cry of our churches. The first is, *"We need finance"* and the second is, *"We need trained workers who*

understands the terrain." The second problem is without doubt the greatest challenge.

Workers in rural settings often labour in areas where the Church is either very young or nonexistent. As a result there is little or no Christian heritage to draw upon. In places where the gospel has been preached for many years, there is no shortage of people who have a basic understanding of Christian principles. People who serve in rural areas cannot compare the progress of their work with those places where there has been a strong Christian heritage.

New converts in rural situations are the next generation of leadership. The way these are viewed determines whether the work will be effective in the long term. The Bible knowledge of young leaders may be limited. But who needs sophisticated Bible expositors in rural situations? In most cases the young leaders will be just a few steps ahead of the people in their Church.

REFERENCES

Abraham, William. *The Logic of Evangelism*. Grand Rapids: Eerdmans, 1989.

Anderson, Alan. *Pentecostalism; The Enlightenment and Christian Mission in Europe*. Cambridge: Goliath, 2004.

Arias, Mortimer. *Announcing the Reign of God: Evangelization and the Subversive Memory of Jesus*. Philadelphia: Fortress, 1984.

Armstrong, Richard Stoll. *Service Evangelism*. Philadelphia: Westminster, 1979.

Banister, Doug. *The Word and Power Church*. Grand Rapids; Zondervan, 1999.

Barth, Karl. *Church Dogmatics*. Edinburgh: T & T Clark, 2004. Biederwolf, William E. *Evangelism: Its Justification, Its Operation and Its Value*. New York: Revell, 1921

Bloesch, Donald G. *The Reform of the Church*. Grand Rapids: Eerdmans, 1970.

Cepenkov, Marko. *Sobrani Dela od Makedonskata Kultura* [Selected Folklore materials]. Skopje: Makedonska Kniga, 1967.

Graham, Billy, Recovering the Primacy of Evangelism. *Christianity Today*, December 8, 1997, Vol. 41, No. 14; 7-12 Petreski 19 Kalajliev, Krum. Personal Interview. Prilep, 15 July 1967.

Klaiber, Walter. *Call and Response: Biblical Foundations of a Theology of Evangelism*. Nashville: Abingdon, 1997.

Kraft, Charles H. *Christianity in Culture*. Maryknoll, NY: Orbis, 1979.

Logan, James C. *Theology and Evangelism in the Wesleyan Heritage.* Nashville: Abingdon, 1993.

Madeley, John T. *European Liberal Democracy and the Principle of State Religious Neutrality,* Oxford: U.P, 1980.

Magrini, Tullia. *Music and Gender: Perspectives from the Mediterranean.* Chicago: U.P, 2003.

Maier, Hans. *Europe's Churches after the Fall of the Walls: European Legacy.* Munich: Ludwig Maximilians Univerisytät, 1998.

Paul, Martin J. *Christianity and Islam: Lessons from Africa,* Polo, UT:
Brigham Young Un. Law Review, January 1998.
Perica, Vjekoslav. *Balkan Idols, Religion and Nationalism in Yugoslav* States. New York: Oxford U P, 2002.

Draft of Final Message of African Synod. African Synod (2009),

The Community of Traditional Values in the African Society: Owerri: Total Publishers Ltd. Aligwekwe.(1991),